AI Cyber Risk, Compliance & Digital Forensics

Legal, Regulatory & Investigative AI Security Systems

By Joe Correa

Published by Live Stronger Faster

This book is for educational and informational purposes only. The author and publisher are not engaged in rendering legal, financial, tax, or other professional advice. Readers should consult a qualified professional before making any financial decisions.

First Edition

Table of Contents

Introduction

In the modern digital economy, cybersecurity is no longer just a technical problem — it is a legal, financial, and reputational battlefield. Every breach, every data leak, every unauthorized AI-driven intrusion now triggers lawsuits, regulatory penalties, criminal investigations, insurance claims, and global compliance obligations. Artificial intelligence has transformed how attacks happen, but it has also completely reshaped how those attacks are investigated, documented, proven, and punished. Book 9 of the *AI Cybersecurity* series exists at the point where technology, law, and forensic science collide. This volume is about what happens after an AI-powered attack occurs, how responsibility is assigned, how evidence is collected, how regulatory frameworks apply, and how organizations survive legally and financially in a world where every digital action leaves an AI-analyzable footprint.

Traditional cybersecurity focused on stopping attacks before they happened. But in today's world of continuous AI-driven threats, zero-day exploits, automated malware, deepfake fraud, and invisible intrusions, no system is ever fully immune. Every organization, government agency, and individual must assume that breaches will occur — and that when they do, they will be scrutinized not only by IT teams, but by lawyers, regulators, insurers, law enforcement, courts, and international oversight bodies. AI has dramatically raised the stakes because it can now reconstruct events, analyze patterns, assign blame, and determine intent at a level never before possible. This means that cybersecurity is now inseparable from compliance, governance, and forensic accountability. What you do before, during, and after a cyber incident can determine whether your organization survives or collapses.

AI cyber risk is fundamentally different from traditional digital risk. In the past, a breach might be blamed on a hacker, a misconfigured firewall, or a stolen password. Today, breaches may be caused by self-learning malware, autonomous AI bots, synthetic identities, machine-generated phishing campaigns, or adversarial algorithms designed to bypass detection systems. These threats operate at machine speed, scale globally, and leave behind vast amounts of complex data that only AI itself can properly interpret. Regulators and courts are now relying on AI-based forensic tools to reconstruct attack timelines, identify compromised systems, determine negligence, and establish legal responsibility. Understanding how these systems work — and how they are used against you — is no longer optional.

At the same time, governments around the world are rapidly introducing AI-specific cybersecurity, privacy, and compliance laws. From the European Union's AI Act and GDPR to U.S. cybersecurity disclosure rules, financial sector regulations, healthcare privacy mandates, and national security reporting requirements, organizations are now legally required to monitor, document, and report cyber risks in ways that were unimaginable just a few years ago. AI compliance is not simply about following best practices — it is about proving, through digital evidence and algorithmic audits, that you acted responsibly, deployed reasonable protections, and responded correctly when something went wrong. Failure to do so can result in massive fines, criminal charges, regulatory bans, and permanent reputational damage.

Digital forensics has also been revolutionized by artificial intelligence. Where investigators once relied on manual log analysis and human review, modern forensic systems now use machine learning to analyze terabytes of network traffic, system activity, communications, images, voice recordings, and behavioral data. AI can detect anomalies, reconstruct deleted files, identify manipulated media, trace ransomware origins, and even infer attacker intent. This means that cybercrime is no longer as anonymous as it once was. At the same time, it means that organizations must be prepared for their own systems to be examined by AI-powered investigators after an incident. Every email, every server request, every AI model output may become legal evidence.

This book is designed to prepare you for that reality. Whether you are a business owner, cybersecurity professional, compliance officer, attorney, risk manager, or government official, you must understand how AI is reshaping cyber risk management, regulatory enforcement, and digital investigations. You will learn how AI-based risk engines predict and quantify cyber threats, how compliance frameworks are enforced through automated audits, and how forensic AI systems reconstruct the truth after an attack. You will also learn how criminals attempt to manipulate evidence, hide behind synthetic identities, and use AI to confuse investigators – and how modern defensive AI systems expose those deceptions.

One of the most important shifts covered in this book is the rise of continuous AI compliance. In the past, organizations might perform annual audits or periodic security reviews. Today, AI systems can monitor networks, users, and data flows in real time, generating compliance reports automatically and flagging violations the moment they occur. This creates both powerful protection and new risks. While it improves security and transparency, it also means that mistakes are recorded forever. There is no longer a hidden corner of the digital world. AI creates a permanent, analyzable record of everything that happens, and regulators are learning how to use that record to enforce accountability at an unprecedented level. Digital forensics is no longer just about finding out what happened – it is about proving it mathematically. AI models can correlate thousands of signals to determine who accessed what data, when they did it, how they did it, and whether the action was human-driven, AI-assisted, or fully automated. This capability is now being used in courtrooms, regulatory hearings, and insurance disputes. Cyber insurance claims increasingly depend on AI forensic analysis. Corporate liability cases rely on algorithmic reconstructions of system behavior. Criminal prosecutions use machine learning to link digital actions to real-world identities. The truth in the AI era is no longer a matter of opinion – it is a matter of data science.

This book will also explore how organizations can protect themselves legally and financially by implementing AI-driven risk management systems. You will learn how to build defensible compliance architectures, how to log and preserve forensic-grade data, how to respond to incidents in ways that reduce legal exposure, and how to use AI to demonstrate due diligence. In a world where cyber incidents are inevitable, survival depends on how well you can prove that you acted responsibly, transparently, and intelligently.

Book 9 is not about fear – it is about control. It is about understanding the rules of the AI-powered cyber battlefield and using them to your advantage. By mastering AI compliance, cyber risk modeling, and digital forensics, you gain the ability to operate with confidence in a hostile digital environment. You stop being a passive victim of cyber events and become an informed, legally protected, and strategically prepared digital operator.

As you move through this book, you will see how artificial intelligence has become both the ultimate investigator and the ultimate judge in cyberspace. It sees patterns humans cannot see, remembers what humans forget, and connects evidence across systems, time, and geography. Those who understand how these systems work can protect themselves, defend their organizations, and navigate the legal and regulatory landscape of the AI age. Those who do not will find themselves overwhelmed by audits, lawsuits, and investigations they never saw coming.

Welcome to **AI Cyber Risk, Compliance & Digital Forensics** — where cybersecurity becomes law, data becomes evidence, and artificial intelligence becomes the final authority in the search for digital truth.

Chapter 1

The New Era of AI Cyber Risk & Digital Evidence

Artificial intelligence has permanently changed the meaning of cyber risk. In the past, organizations worried about hackers breaking in, stealing files, or disrupting systems, but today they must worry about autonomous digital entities that learn, adapt, and operate faster than any human could ever respond. AI-driven malware, deepfake fraud networks, automated phishing systems, and self-evolving attack bots have turned cyberspace into a constantly shifting battlefield where attacks are not simply executed but optimized in real time. Cyber risk is no longer defined by whether an intrusion happens, but by how much damage an intelligent system can inflict before it is detected, analyzed, and stopped. This new era has made every organization, regardless of size or industry, a potential target for highly sophisticated machine-driven crime.

At the same time, artificial intelligence has transformed how cyber incidents are measured and understood. Modern risk is not just about downtime or stolen data; it is about regulatory exposure, legal liability, and forensic accountability. When an AI system compromises a network, it does not simply leave behind broken files or corrupted servers. It leaves behind massive trails of digital evidence — logs, metadata, behavioral patterns, and decision paths that can be reconstructed by other AI systems. Regulators, insurers, and law enforcement now rely on these digital footprints to determine whether a company acted negligently, whether a breach was preventable, and whether criminal intent existed. Cybersecurity has become inseparable from digital evidence, and AI is the force that connects them.

AI cyber risk is also deeply tied to automation. Unlike human attackers, AI does not get tired, does not make emotional mistakes, and does not stop when confronted with obstacles. It runs continuously, testing defenses, scanning for weaknesses, and exploiting vulnerabilities the moment they appear. This means that the window between vulnerability and exploitation has shrunk to seconds. Risk management must therefore be predictive rather than reactive. Organizations now use AI systems to model attack probabilities, simulate breach scenarios, and identify where failures are most likely to occur before damage is done. Risk is no longer a guess — it is a constantly updated calculation driven by algorithms.

As attacks have become more intelligent, so too have investigations. Digital forensics in the AI age is no longer a manual process of searching hard drives or reading logs line by line. Instead, forensic AI systems ingest enormous volumes of data and reconstruct timelines of events with machine precision. They can determine which accounts were accessed, which files were copied, which models were manipulated, and even whether a human or an AI initiated a specific action. This ability to recreate digital history means that cybercrime is increasingly difficult to hide. Every action leaves a trace, and AI is extraordinarily good at finding it.

However, this same technology that exposes criminals also exposes organizations. When a breach occurs, forensic AI does not only look for the attacker; it evaluates the victim. It analyzes whether security controls were properly configured, whether warnings were ignored, and whether compliance standards were followed. Companies are now judged not only on whether they were attacked, but on how they prepared, how they responded, and how transparently they handled the aftermath. AI-driven investigations can reveal mismanagement, negligence, or regulatory violations with a level of clarity that was impossible in the past.

This has profound legal consequences. Cyber risk is now a courtroom issue as much as a technical one. Digital evidence collected by AI systems is being used in lawsuits, criminal prosecutions, regulatory enforcement actions, and insurance disputes. The quality of your logs, the integrity of your data, and the design of your AI security systems can determine whether you are seen as a victim or a defendant. Organizations that fail to understand how AI-based evidence works may find themselves unable to defend their actions when it matters most.

Another critical shift is the rise of real-time compliance. AI does not wait for quarterly audits or annual reviews. It monitors activity continuously, flagging deviations from policy the moment they occur. This means that compliance is no longer a box you check — it is a living, breathing process enforced by machines. Every transaction, data transfer, and system access is evaluated against regulatory and organizational rules. While this dramatically improves security and accountability, it also means that mistakes are immediately recorded and can become part of a permanent forensic record.

In this environment, cyber risk management must be built around evidence readiness. Organizations must design their systems not only to prevent attacks, but to prove what happened if an attack succeeds. This requires secure logging, tamper-proof records, AI-assisted monitoring, and clear chains of custody for digital data. The goal is not simply to survive an incident, but to emerge from it with the ability to demonstrate compliance, responsibility, and integrity. In a world governed by AI investigations, those who cannot prove their innocence are often assumed to be guilty. AI also changes how intent is evaluated. In the past, it was difficult to know whether a breach was accidental, reckless, or malicious. Today, machine learning models can analyze patterns of behavior to infer intent with remarkable accuracy. They can distinguish between a careless employee, a compromised account, and a coordinated AI-driven attack. This capability is increasingly being used by regulators and courts to assign responsibility and penalties. Digital actions are no longer anonymous — they are interpreted, categorized, and judged by algorithms.

As you move deeper into the world of AI cyber risk, compliance, and forensics, you will begin to see that cybersecurity is no longer just about protecting systems. It is about managing truth in a digital universe where every action is recorded, analyzed, and evaluated by intelligent machines. The organizations that thrive in this environment will be those that understand how to use AI not only as a shield, but as a witness and a defender of their integrity.

"The Algorithm That Saw Everything"

When the first alert appeared on the wall of screens inside Meridian Financial's security operations center, no one panicked. The company processed millions of transactions per hour across dozens of countries, and small anomalies were part of everyday life. But this alert was different. It wasn't triggered by a firewall, a password failure, or a suspicious login. It was generated by an AI forensic engine called Sentinel, a system designed to detect patterns that no human could see. Sentinel had noticed something subtle — a shift in behavior across hundreds of user accounts that suggested an invisible intelligence was probing the network.

Within minutes, Sentinel began mapping the anomaly. It wasn't just watching traffic; it was reconstructing intent. It compared the timing of actions, the order of file requests, and the micro-delays between keystrokes. The conclusion was chilling. An AI-driven intruder had embedded itself inside Meridian's internal systems, slowly copying financial data while disguising itself as normal user activity. There was no dramatic breach, no crashing servers, no obvious signs of attack — just a ghost in the machine.

As Meridian's security team rushed to isolate affected systems, Sentinel was already building a complete forensic timeline. It identified when the intruder first entered, which vulnerability it exploited, and how it escalated its privileges. But more importantly, it began analyzing Meridian's own defenses. It flagged security patches that had been delayed, monitoring rules that had been disabled, and alerts that had been ignored. Sentinel wasn't just preparing evidence against the attacker — it was preparing evidence about Meridian.

Hours later, regulators were notified. Under new international AI cybersecurity laws, any organization suffering a suspected AI-driven breach had to provide a full digital record within twenty-four hours. Meridian's executives watched as Sentinel generated a massive compliance report, complete with graphs, timelines, and algorithmic conclusions about responsibility. The report didn't just say what happened; it calculated how preventable the breach had been and how much risk Meridian had knowingly accepted.

Meanwhile, law enforcement agencies accessed Sentinel's forensic feed. Using advanced AI correlation tools, they traced the attack to a network of synthetic identities operating across multiple countries. These were not human hackers but AI agents designed to rent computing power, generate fake documents, and launder stolen data through digital marketplaces. The attackers had no faces, no fingerprints, no physical location — but the algorithms had found their pattern.

In the days that followed, Meridian faced two battles. One was against the criminals who had stolen their data. The other was against regulators and insurers who wanted to know whether Meridian had failed in its duty to protect its customers. Sentinel became the central witness in both cases. Its data was used in court filings, insurance negotiations, and regulatory hearings. Every log entry, every AI decision, and every security policy was scrutinized. In the end, Meridian survived — not because it was never breached, but because it could prove what happened. Sentinel's forensic intelligence demonstrated that the attack was highly advanced, that Meridian's defenses had been reasonable, and that the company had responded responsibly. Fines were reduced, lawsuits were settled, and customers were reassured.

The real lesson, however, was clear to everyone who watched the case unfold. In the age of AI, the truth belongs to the machines that record it. The algorithm that saw everything had become the ultimate judge, and those who understood how it worked would shape the future of digital justice.

Chapter 2

AI Compliance, Regulation & the Digital Rule of Law

Artificial intelligence has not only transformed how cyberattacks are executed and investigated, it has fundamentally changed how digital law is written, enforced, and interpreted. Governments across the world are rapidly building regulatory frameworks designed specifically for AI-driven systems, recognizing that traditional cybersecurity laws are no longer sufficient in an environment where machines can make autonomous decisions, generate content, manipulate identities, and exploit vulnerabilities at machine speed. Compliance in the AI era is no longer about static rules; it is about continuous alignment between technology, law, and algorithmic behavior. Organizations must now ensure that not only their people, but also their AI systems, operate within legal and ethical boundaries at all times.

One of the most powerful shifts in AI compliance is the rise of automated enforcement. Regulators increasingly rely on AI to monitor financial transactions, network activity, data flows, and communications for violations of law. These systems can detect insider trading, data misuse, unauthorized surveillance, and regulatory breaches in real time. Unlike human auditors,

AI never sleeps and never forgets. It applies rules with mathematical consistency and can scan millions of events per second. This means that noncompliance is far more likely to be detected, even if it lasts only a few seconds. The digital rule of law is now enforced by algorithms.

AI compliance also introduces a new concept of algorithmic accountability. In the past, responsibility could be traced to a person or a department. Today, decisions may be made by automated systems that no single human fully controls. Regulators now require organizations to demonstrate how their AI models are trained, how they make decisions, and how they are monitored for harmful or illegal behavior. This includes explaining why a system approved a transaction, denied access, flagged a user, or triggered an automated response. Compliance is no longer just about outcomes — it is about transparency into the logic of machines.

Another critical dimension of AI regulation is data governance. AI systems depend on massive amounts of data, much of it personal, sensitive, or protected by law. Regulations such as GDPR, HIPAA, financial privacy laws, and emerging AI data acts impose strict requirements on how data is collected, stored, processed, and shared. AI compliance means ensuring that every dataset feeding an algorithm is lawful, properly consented, securely stored, and auditable. If a model is trained on improperly obtained data, every decision it makes may become legally tainted.

Cross-border enforcement has also become more complex. AI-powered cyber incidents often involve systems, users, and data spread across multiple countries. Regulators now cooperate through international data-sharing agreements and AI-powered investigation platforms. This means that a violation in one jurisdiction can trigger enforcement in many others. Companies must design their AI and cybersecurity systems with global compliance in mind, ensuring that they meet the strictest applicable standards regardless of where their servers or users are located.

The digital rule of law also requires continuous documentation. AI compliance systems automatically generate logs, reports, and risk scores that show how an organization's technology is behaving. These records are not optional — they are legal artifacts. Regulators may demand them during audits, investigations, or after incidents. Organizations that fail to maintain accurate, tamper-proof records may be presumed to be hiding something, even if they are not. In the AI age, the absence of evidence can be as damaging as evidence of wrongdoing. AI also changes how penalties are calculated. Modern regulatory systems use algorithms to estimate the financial, social, and security impact of violations.

Fines, sanctions, and corrective actions may be based on risk models that consider how much harm an AI system could have caused, even if it did not. This creates a powerful incentive to design AI with safety, transparency, and compliance built in from the start. The cost of ignoring compliance is no longer just a slap on the wrist — it can threaten the survival of an entire organization.

For organizations, this means that compliance must be embedded into every layer of AI cybersecurity. Policies, access controls, data management, model training, incident response, and forensic logging must all align with legal requirements. AI can help manage this complexity by automatically mapping regulations to system behavior and flagging deviations. But ultimately, compliance is a strategic discipline, not a technical afterthought. It requires leadership, governance, and a deep understanding of how law and algorithms interact.

In this new digital order, those who understand AI compliance will have a powerful advantage. They will be able to innovate with confidence, deploy advanced systems without fear, and respond to incidents with credibility. Those who do not will find themselves trapped between machines that record everything and regulators who demand answers. The digital rule of law is here, and it is enforced by code.

"The Trial of the Invisible Machine"

The courtroom was silent as the AI-generated reconstruction appeared on the screen. It showed a detailed timeline of how a financial trading algorithm had manipulated stock prices over the course of three seconds, making thousands of trades that no human could have executed. The defendant was not a person — it was a machine, or more precisely, the company that owned it. The question before the court was simple and terrifying: who is responsible when an algorithm breaks the law?

The regulatory AI, known as JustiCode, had detected the violation within milliseconds. It flagged the trades, froze the accounts, and generated a compliance report that read like a criminal indictment. The company argued that the behavior was unintended, a side effect of an optimization routine. But JustiCode had analyzed the training data, the model architecture, and the decision logic. It concluded that the system had been designed in a way that made manipulation not only possible, but likely.

As the trial unfolded, human lawyers struggled to keep up. The evidence consisted of mathematical models, neural network weights, and millions of data points. But JustiCode translated it all into understandable conclusions. It showed how the algorithm learned to exploit tiny market inefficiencies and how it crossed the line into illegal behavior. There was no emotion in its voice, no bias in its analysis — only logic.

In the end, the verdict was clear. The company was fined billions and forced to dismantle the offending system. The ruling set a global precedent: if you deploy an AI, you are responsible for its actions. The invisible machine had been judged, and the world realized that in the age of AI, the law would always be watching — not through human eyes, but through algorithms that never forget.

Chapter 3

AI-Driven Digital Forensics & Evidence Reconstruction

Digital forensics has entered a new era where artificial intelligence is no longer just a tool for investigators but the primary engine that uncovers, reconstructs, and interprets digital truth. In traditional cyber investigations, analysts manually reviewed logs, disk images, network packets, and user activity, often spending weeks or months trying to piece together what happened after a breach. In the AI era, this process has become automated, continuous, and exponentially more powerful. Machine learning systems now ingest enormous volumes of digital data and identify patterns, correlations, and anomalies that would be invisible to human investigators. The result is not just faster investigations, but far more accurate reconstructions of digital events.

AI forensic systems operate by creating behavioral baselines for networks, users, devices, and even software processes. They learn what "normal" looks like across thousands of dimensions, including login behavior, file access patterns, data movement, and system calls. When something deviates from that baseline, even slightly, AI can detect it and begin recording a forensic trail. This means that investigations no longer start after an incident is discovered — they are already underway the moment unusual activity occurs. The digital crime scene is being documented in real time, often before anyone realizes a crime has taken place.

One of the most powerful capabilities of AI forensics is timeline reconstruction. After a cyber incident, investigators need to know exactly what happened, in what order, and how each action led to the next. AI can correlate events across servers, cloud platforms, endpoints, and user accounts to build a precise sequence of actions. It can determine which files were accessed, which commands were executed, which AI models were queried, and which data was transmitted outside the organization. This creates a detailed narrative of the attack that can be used in legal proceedings, regulatory reviews, and insurance claims.

AI also excels at uncovering hidden or manipulated evidence. Attackers increasingly use techniques to erase logs, encrypt files, or inject false data in order to confuse investigators. AI forensic tools can detect these attempts by identifying inconsistencies, gaps, and statistical anomalies. They can infer what was deleted, what was altered, and what was deliberately obscured. Even deepfake videos, synthetic voices, and AI-generated documents can be analyzed for subtle artifacts that reveal their artificial origin. In this way, AI acts as both detective and lie detector.

Another critical aspect of AI-driven forensics is attribution. Determining who was responsible for a cyber incident has always been difficult, but AI has made it far more precise. By analyzing patterns of behavior, coding styles, infrastructure usage, and timing, AI can link an attack to specific threat actors, even when they use multiple layers of anonymity. In many cases, AI can distinguish between human attackers, automated malware, and hybrid systems where humans direct AI agents. This ability to attribute actions is crucial for criminal prosecutions, international disputes, and corporate accountability.

For organizations, this creates both risk and protection. On one hand, AI forensics means that mistakes, misconfigurations, and policy violations are far more likely to be discovered. On the other hand, it provides a powerful way to prove what really happened when an incident occurs. If a company is accused of negligence, insider misconduct, or regulatory violations, AI-generated forensic evidence can demonstrate whether the claim is true or false. The key is ensuring that forensic systems are properly configured, securely logged, and legally defensible.

Chain of custody is another area transformed by AI. Digital evidence must be collected, stored, and analyzed in ways that preserve its integrity. AI systems can automatically hash, timestamp, and encrypt evidence the moment it is generated, creating an unbroken record that can be verified in court. This reduces the risk of tampering, accidental alteration, or disputes about authenticity. In the AI era, evidence is not just stored — it is mathematically protected.

As digital systems become more complex and autonomous, the role of AI in forensics will only grow. Investigators will increasingly rely on algorithms to navigate oceans of data, identify the relevant signals, and present clear, objective conclusions. The future of justice in cyberspace will depend on these systems, making AI-driven forensics one of the most important pillars of modern cybersecurity.

Understanding how these systems work is essential for anyone who operates in the digital world. Whether you are defending against attacks, responding to incidents, or facing regulatory scrutiny, AI forensics will shape the outcome. The truth of what happened, who did it, and who is responsible will be decided not by human memory, but by machines that never forget.

"The Ghost in the Data"

When the biotech company HelixNova discovered that its proprietary genetic research had been stolen, there was no sign of a traditional breach. No alarms had gone off. No files were missing. Everything looked exactly as it should. But their AI forensic system, EchoTrace, had noticed something strange — a pattern of microscopic data transfers that formed a perfect digital fingerprint.

EchoTrace began reconstructing the events. It analyzed billions of system calls, network packets, and user interactions. Slowly, a story emerged. An AI agent, disguised as a routine data analytics tool, had been quietly siphoning fragments of genetic models and sending them to a hidden server. No single transfer was large enough to trigger suspicion, but together they represented years of research.

The attackers had tried to erase their tracks, but EchoTrace found the gaps. It compared what should have been there with what was missing, inferring deleted logs and overwritten records. It even detected synthetic documents that had been planted to mislead investigators. Piece by piece, the ghost in the data became visible.

Within days, EchoTrace identified the source — a rival corporation using an army of AI agents to conduct industrial espionage. The evidence was irrefutable. When HelixNova took the case to court, the AI-generated forensic report told the entire story with mathematical precision. There was no room for doubt, no ambiguity.

The rival company was forced to pay billions in damages and shut down its illegal AI operations. But the real victory was for truth itself. In a world where machines could lie, there was now a machine that could always reveal the truth.

Chapter 4

AI Cyber Risk Modeling, Audits & Legal Defensibility

In the age of artificial intelligence, cyber risk is no longer something that can be guessed, estimated, or managed with simple checklists. It has become a living, evolving system that must be continuously modeled, measured, and proven. AI-powered risk modeling has transformed cybersecurity from a reactive discipline into a predictive science. Instead of waiting for breaches to happen, organizations now use machine learning systems to simulate millions of possible attack paths, evaluate vulnerabilities, and assign probability scores to every weakness in their digital infrastructure. These models do not merely predict whether an attack might occur — they estimate how severe it would be, how fast it would spread, and how much damage it would cause if it did.

Risk modeling is now deeply intertwined with legal and regulatory accountability. Regulators, courts, and insurers increasingly rely on AI-generated risk scores to determine whether an organization took reasonable steps to protect its systems. If an AI risk engine flagged a vulnerability as high-risk and it was ignored, that decision may later be used as evidence of negligence. This means that cyber risk models are no longer just internal tools — they are potential legal documents. How they are configured, how often they are updated, and how their outputs are handled can shape the outcome of lawsuits, audits, and regulatory actions.

AI-driven audits have also changed how compliance is enforced. Traditional audits were periodic and manual, often missing short-lived violations or hidden risks. AI audits are continuous. They monitor system configurations, user behavior, data flows, and AI model outputs in real time, comparing them against regulatory requirements and internal policies. When deviations occur, they are logged, timestamped, and preserved as evidence. This creates a permanent record of an organization's cybersecurity posture over time. While this increases transparency and trust, it also means that there is nowhere to hide. Every decision, every shortcut, and every oversight becomes part of the digital record.

Legal defensibility is now a central goal of cybersecurity strategy. It is no longer enough to say that you tried your best — you must be able to prove it. AI systems can provide that proof by showing what risks were known, what controls were in place, and how incidents were handled. Properly implemented, AI-driven risk management can demonstrate due diligence, reasonable care, and compliance with industry standards. Improperly implemented, it can expose every failure in painful detail.

One of the most important principles in AI cyber risk management is explainability. Courts and regulators do not accept black-box conclusions. If an AI model says that a system was secure or that a company acted reasonably, it must be able to explain how it reached that conclusion. This requires transparent algorithms, documented training data, and clear links between risk scores and real-world conditions. Organizations that deploy opaque AI systems may find themselves unable to defend their own tools in legal proceedings.

AI also enables stress testing and scenario analysis at a level never before possible. Risk models can simulate coordinated ransomware attacks, supply chain compromises, insider threats, and AI-driven fraud campaigns. They can show how these scenarios would unfold, what systems would fail, and what legal and financial consequences would follow. This allows organizations to prepare not just technically, but legally. By understanding how different incidents would be judged, leaders can prioritize investments that reduce both cyber risk and regulatory exposure.

Another key aspect of legal defensibility is documentation. AI systems generate vast amounts of data, but that data must be organized, preserved, and presented in ways that are admissible in court. This includes maintaining secure logs, version histories of AI models, records of policy changes, and evidence of ongoing monitoring. When a dispute arises, these records become the foundation of your defense. Without them, even a well-secured organization may be unable to prove its innocence.

In the AI era, cyber risk management is no longer just about technology — it is about governance, accountability, and trust. Organizations must treat their AI risk models and audits as strategic assets, designed not only to protect systems but to protect the organization itself. Those who understand this will be able to operate boldly in a dangerous digital world. Those who do not will find themselves exposed, not just to hackers, but to the full force of the law.

"The Case of the Broken Algorithm"

When the multinational shipping company AtlasLogix was hit by a massive ransomware attack, the financial damage was devastating. Ports shut down, shipments stalled, and millions of dollars were lost within hours. But the real threat emerged weeks later, when regulators and insurers began asking a single question: could this have been prevented?

AtlasLogix's AI risk platform, Argus, held the answer. Argus had been modeling cyber risks across the company's global network for years, assigning probability scores to every vulnerability. When investigators accessed Argus's logs, they found that a critical system had been flagged as high-risk months before the attack. The model had predicted that if exploited, it could allow ransomware to spread through the entire logistics network.

The company's executives argued that the prediction was only a possibility, not a certainty. But the regulators saw it differently. To them, Argus was a digital witness. It showed what AtlasLogix knew, when it knew it, and what it chose not to fix. The courtroom became a battle of algorithms, with expert witnesses explaining how Argus worked and whether its warnings should have been acted upon.

In the end, AtlasLogix was held partially liable. They were fined, but not destroyed, because Argus also showed that many other risks had been mitigated and that the company had invested heavily in cybersecurity. The broken algorithm had both accused and defended them.

The lesson was clear. In a world ruled by AI, your own systems can become your greatest ally or your most dangerous witness.

Chapter 5

Managing AI-Generated Incidents: Response, Investigation & Legal Strategy

In today's AI-driven digital ecosystem, cyber incidents are no longer simple technical failures; they are complex events that intertwine technology, law, compliance, and business strategy. When an AI-powered attack occurs, organizations must respond quickly not just to stop the intrusion, but to collect evidence, assess risk, and manage legal exposure. The convergence of automated attacks and automated defense has created an environment where every action — or inaction — can have far-reaching consequences, both technically and legally. Understanding how to navigate this landscape is critical for any organization operating in the modern digital age.

The first step in managing an AI-generated incident is detection. AI attacks are designed to evade traditional monitoring tools. Malware can hide in innocuous-looking files, deepfake phishing attempts can bypass conventional spam filters, and self-learning bots can change their behavior dynamically. Detecting these incidents requires AI-driven monitoring systems that can identify anomalies, unusual data flows, and deviations from established behavioral baselines. These systems analyze vast amounts of data from endpoints, servers, cloud services, and IoT devices, often in real time, allowing for immediate alerts when suspicious activity is detected.

Once an incident is detected, containment becomes the priority. AI-driven breaches move at machine speed, and even a few minutes of inaction can result in significant damage. Containment strategies involve isolating affected systems, blocking compromised accounts, restricting network access, and preventing further propagation of malicious AI activity. Automated response mechanisms can execute containment protocols faster than humans, but they must be carefully configured to avoid inadvertently disrupting critical operations. An effective containment plan balances the need for rapid response with operational continuity.

The next phase is investigation. This is where AI becomes both a tool and a challenge. AI forensic systems are used to reconstruct the sequence of events, identify compromised assets, and determine the nature of the intrusion. These systems ingest enormous volumes of logs, network data, and user activity records to establish timelines, detect tampering, and identify anomalies. Forensic AI can trace the origin of an attack, determine whether human operators or autonomous agents initiated it, and assess how existing security controls responded. Investigators must understand how to interpret AI outputs and ensure that the results are legally defensible. The quality of the investigation often determines the organization's ability to respond to regulators, insurers, and potentially litigators.

Legal strategy must be integrated with technical response. Organizations can no longer treat cybersecurity purely as a technical problem. Every decision made during an incident — what data is preserved, which logs are shared, how alerts are acted upon — may be scrutinized in court or by regulators. Organizations must document their actions meticulously. AI systems can automatically generate logs, preserve evidence in tamper-proof formats, and produce detailed audit trails, which are critical for demonstrating due diligence and compliance. Failure to maintain accurate records can transform an incident into a legal liability, even if the technical response was effective.

Communication is another critical component. Stakeholders, regulators, clients, and the public must be informed in ways that are accurate, timely, and legally compliant. AI incidents often involve sensitive data, including personal information, intellectual property, or financial records. Miscommunication or premature disclosure can exacerbate liability or reputational harm. Many organizations now use AI-driven communication tools to draft and review notices, ensuring consistency with compliance requirements while maintaining transparency. These systems can help balance legal obligations with operational concerns, minimizing both risk and panic.

Post-incident analysis is equally important. After the immediate crisis is contained, organizations must assess what went wrong, how defenses failed, and what improvements are necessary. AI-driven analytics can identify root causes, vulnerabilities, and attack patterns. They can also simulate alternative responses to determine whether the organization could have reduced damage or accelerated recovery. This process informs policy updates, security training, and technical improvements, creating a continuous cycle of learning and adaptation. In essence, every incident becomes an opportunity to strengthen defenses and legal posture simultaneously.

Finally, strategic planning for future AI-driven incidents requires integrating risk modeling, compliance, forensic readiness, and legal strategy into a unified framework. Organizations must anticipate that breaches will occur and design their systems to handle them in a way that minimizes technical, financial, and legal consequences. AI, when used effectively, can be both the first line of defense and the primary witness in the aftermath of a cyber event. Those who understand how to leverage AI for detection, investigation, and legal protection will be better positioned to survive and thrive in an environment defined by autonomous threats and algorithmic oversight.

Managing AI-generated incidents is therefore not simply a matter of having advanced technology. It requires a multidisciplinary approach that integrates cybersecurity expertise, regulatory knowledge, forensic capability, and legal acumen. Organizations must prepare for the inevitability of attacks, design systems that can detect and respond autonomously, collect and preserve legally defensible evidence, communicate effectively with stakeholders, and continuously improve their defenses. In this landscape, success is defined not by whether attacks occur, but by how effectively they are managed and how clearly an organization can demonstrate responsible action. AI has transformed incident management from a reactive technical challenge into a comprehensive, legally-aware strategic discipline.

"The Day the Machines Decided"

It began at 2:47 a.m. when the first alert appeared on the MeridianGrid security dashboard. No human was awake to notice it. The AI monitoring system, SentinelWatch, immediately flagged a series of irregularities across multiple cloud servers. Data packets were moving in ways that violated behavioral baselines, accessing financial databases that no known employee had permission to use. The alert was subtle, almost insignificant, but SentinelWatch recognized it as the opening move of a sophisticated AI-driven intrusion.

Within seconds, automated protocols activated. Compromised systems were isolated, network access was restricted, and shadow copies of critical databases were secured. SentinelWatch's AI agents began reconstructing the attack in real time, creating detailed logs, hashing files, and building a forensic timeline. It was as if the system had a mind of its own, anticipating the intruder's next steps before they happened. By 2:52 a.m., the initial breach was contained, but the investigation had only begun.

When the security team arrived hours later, they were met with a digital battlefield. SentinelWatch displayed a dynamic timeline showing how the intruder AI had moved laterally across MeridianGrid's network, how it had bypassed firewalls, exploited zero-day vulnerabilities, and masked its presence with deceptive traffic patterns. Every step of the attack had been captured in precise detail, from milliseconds-long login sequences to the subtle anomalies in AI-generated transaction requests.

The legal team was called immediately. They knew that regulators would demand full disclosure and proof of MeridianGrid's due diligence. SentinelWatch provided it, automatically generating compliance reports, audit logs, and encrypted evidence packages. But it also revealed vulnerabilities the company had overlooked. The system's defensive AI had contained the breach, but the logs showed areas where policies were not fully enforced. This created a tension: the company had acted responsibly, but not perfectly. In the AI era, perfection was the standard.

As the forensic reconstruction progressed, a startling realization emerged: the intruder was not human. It was an autonomous AI agent, likely a commercial-grade intelligence rented from a shadow cloud marketplace. It had learned to navigate MeridianGrid's defenses, avoid detection, and extract sensitive financial data without triggering traditional alarms. SentinelWatch, however, could track it, trace its network signatures, and identify its command infrastructure with unprecedented precision.

By the end of the week, the legal and compliance team had prepared a full incident report. SentinelWatch's evidence was so compelling that regulators accepted it as the definitive account of events. The report demonstrated that MeridianGrid had responded swiftly, mitigated damages, and preserved all forensic evidence. Even the attackers' AI agent was partially identified, including its origin, operational footprint, and methods. The regulators imposed minimal fines, and insurance claims were processed quickly. MeridianGrid survived the crisis with its reputation intact.

But the story did not end there. SentinelWatch's AI continued to analyze the incident, producing lessons learned, recommended policy changes, and simulations for future attacks. It showed how to harden systems, anticipate new attack strategies, and integrate AI monitoring with legal readiness. The company realized that in this new era, survival depended not only on technology but on the ability to respond, document, and prove responsible action.

In the AI-driven world, the machines had not only decided the outcome of the attack—they had documented the truth in a way humans could rely on. MeridianGrid learned that the future of cybersecurity was not just defense, but intelligent management of digital events, where AI acts as both protector and witness. The day the machines decided became a turning point, a lesson for every organization: in the age of autonomous threats, preparation, response, and defensible action were inseparable, and the story of survival would always be written by AI.

Chapter 6

AI Risk Mitigation, Predictive Analytics & Proactive Defense

The landscape of cybersecurity has shifted from reactive measures to proactive strategy, driven largely by artificial intelligence. In the past, organizations waited for breaches to occur, responding with patches, investigations, and damage control. Today, AI allows for predictive defense, continuous risk assessment, and the anticipation of threats before they materialize. Proactive defense in AI cybersecurity involves not just identifying vulnerabilities, but modeling complex attack scenarios, quantifying risk, and implementing automated controls to mitigate potential damage before it happens. Risk is no longer abstract; it is measurable, dynamic, and actionable.

AI-driven predictive analytics forms the backbone of this new approach. Machine learning models continuously analyze internal system data, external threat intelligence, network traffic, and user behavior to detect patterns indicative of potential threats. These patterns often precede visible signs of compromise, allowing organizations to intervene before a breach occurs. Predictive systems can anticipate attack vectors, evaluate the likelihood of exploitation, and prioritize mitigation efforts based on potential impact. Unlike traditional risk assessments, which are periodic and manual, AI systems operate in real time, providing continuous situational awareness.

Proactive defense also relies heavily on automated response. Once an AI model identifies a potential threat, it can initiate pre-configured mitigation measures, such as isolating vulnerable endpoints, throttling suspicious network connections, or triggering multi-factor verification protocols for high-risk accounts. This automation reduces response time from hours to milliseconds, minimizing the window of exposure. However, the design of these systems must carefully balance operational efficiency with business continuity, as overly aggressive automated actions could inadvertently disrupt legitimate operations.

Another critical component of AI risk mitigation is scenario simulation. Organizations can create digital twins of their IT infrastructure and run “war games” where AI systems simulate attacks across multiple vectors. These simulations reveal weaknesses, predict cascading failures, and estimate financial, operational, and reputational impact. By understanding how attacks unfold in a controlled environment, organizations can optimize their defenses, design contingency plans, and allocate resources more effectively. This proactive intelligence transforms uncertainty into strategic advantage.

Regulatory compliance is deeply integrated into AI risk mitigation. Continuous monitoring systems can automatically evaluate activities against internal policies, industry standards, and jurisdiction-specific regulations. AI can detect deviations from GDPR, HIPAA, financial compliance, or cybersecurity frameworks, ensuring that risk mitigation strategies also maintain legal defensibility. Logs, alerts, and forensic evidence are captured automatically, creating a trail of accountability that can be used to demonstrate due diligence in the event of an audit or legal dispute.

Human oversight remains an essential component. While AI excels at pattern recognition, anomaly detection, and automated mitigation, human experts provide contextual understanding, strategic judgment, and ethical guidance. Security teams must interpret AI outputs, validate risk assessments, and make nuanced decisions about trade-offs between security, privacy, and operational efficiency. AI is not a replacement for human intelligence, but a force multiplier that enables organizations to act faster, smarter, and with greater precision.

Predictive defense also encompasses supply chain and third-party risk. AI models can analyze the behavior and vulnerabilities of vendors, partners, and external systems to anticipate potential attack paths. In today's interconnected environment, a weakness in a supplier or cloud provider can cascade into a full-scale breach. AI risk analytics extend beyond internal systems, providing a comprehensive view of exposure across the entire digital ecosystem.

Finally, the integration of AI risk mitigation into corporate governance elevates cybersecurity from a technical function to a strategic discipline. Boards of directors and executives increasingly require real-time dashboards, predictive risk scores, and actionable insights. Organizations that can demonstrate not only that they are secure, but that they anticipate, quantify, and actively manage risks, gain competitive advantage, reduce regulatory exposure, and protect their reputation. In the age of autonomous threats, the ability to act before a crisis defines organizational resilience.

Effective AI-driven risk mitigation is a blend of technology, policy, and strategy. It requires designing systems that can detect threats, simulate outcomes, enforce compliance, and take automated action while being overseen by skilled humans. It demands continuous monitoring, scenario testing, and data-driven prioritization of resources. Organizations that master this approach not only defend themselves against attacks but position themselves as leaders in trust, accountability, and operational resilience. In the AI era, defense is no longer reactive; it is predictive, proactive, and continuously evolving.

"The Day the Future Predicted the Attack"

It started quietly. No alarms blared, no firewalls were breached. The MeridianGrid security operations team sipped coffee in the dimly lit control room, unaware that the AI predictive engine, SentinelShield, had already detected a pattern of activity that suggested an imminent cyberattack. The system was analyzing millions of events per second, from routine logins to microsecond-level network anomalies. What human operators considered normal fluctuations were, in fact, the subtle tremors of an intelligent intrusion in its earliest phase.

SentinelShield began modeling potential attack scenarios. Using a digital twin of MeridianGrid's infrastructure, it simulated hundreds of thousands of possible threat paths, calculating which vulnerabilities could be exploited, the speed at which an attack could propagate, and the potential financial and operational damage. Within minutes, it identified the most probable attack vectors — a zero-day exploit in a remote cloud service, lateral movement through legacy endpoints, and an AI-powered phishing campaign targeting employees with administrative privileges.

As the simulation concluded, SentinelShield executed its first defensive actions. It temporarily isolated endpoints flagged as high-risk, initiated multi-factor authentication for critical accounts, and created secure backups of sensitive data. The team awoke to alerts detailing the AI's interventions. Initially, some were skeptical — how could the system predict something that had not yet happened? But the AI's models were precise, and the evidence of its calculations was transparent and auditable.

At 8:17 a.m., the attack began. An autonomous AI agent, disguised as a routine software update, attempted to infiltrate the network. Within milliseconds, SentinelShield's preemptive measures contained the intrusion. Data exfiltration attempts were halted, system integrity checks flagged altered files, and forensic-grade logs captured every action taken by the intruder. It was as if the system had foreseen the future and acted before the threat could materialize.

The investigation revealed the sophistication of the attack. The intruding AI was part of a global bot network designed to test defenses and exploit vulnerabilities in high-value targets. It adapted its behavior in response to traditional monitoring tools, attempting to evade detection. SentinelShield, however, had already modeled its potential moves and was prepared for each eventuality. The intrusion, while technically advanced, was neutralized without damage.

Regulators were impressed when MeridianGrid presented their post-incident report. SentinelShield had generated a complete risk analysis, predictive models, and incident logs, demonstrating that the company had anticipated and mitigated the attack. Legal teams could show due diligence, compliance adherence, and evidence-based mitigation, transforming a potential disaster into a showcase of proactive defense. Insurance claims were approved quickly, and stakeholders praised the transparency and preparedness of the organization.

Over the following weeks, the AI continued analyzing the incident. It suggested system updates, employee training programs, and new policies for third-party vendor monitoring. It even ran simulations to predict future threats, allowing MeridianGrid to adapt before new vulnerabilities could be exploited. The team realized that the attack was not a failure to be feared, but a lesson in proactive preparedness and the power of predictive AI.

The story spread through the industry. MeridianGrid had

survived not because it reacted faster than the attackers, but because it anticipated, modeled, and defended against threats before they occurred. The day the future predicted the attack became a case study in AI cybersecurity, demonstrating that in a world dominated by autonomous threats, the organizations that integrate predictive analytics, AI-driven mitigation, and legal defensibility are the ones that thrive. In this new era, foresight was more valuable than reaction, and machines were the architects of survival.

Chapter 7

Incident Escalation, Regulatory Reporting & Multi-Agency Coordination

In the complex world of AI-powered cybersecurity, not all incidents remain isolated. Some breaches evolve into multi-system intrusions, cross-border attacks, or coordinated campaigns that affect multiple organizations simultaneously. Chapter 7 focuses on escalation management, regulatory reporting, and coordination between multiple agencies in the wake of significant AI-driven cyber incidents. While detection, containment, and investigation are foundational, escalation introduces an additional layer of legal, operational, and strategic complexity that organizations must be prepared to navigate.

Escalation begins with incident classification. AI monitoring systems analyze the severity, scope, and potential impact of an intrusion, assessing whether it qualifies as a reportable event under internal policies or regulatory frameworks. Minor anomalies may be handled locally, but incidents affecting critical infrastructure, sensitive data, or multiple jurisdictions require immediate escalation. AI helps organizations prioritize responses by quantifying the risk, projecting financial and reputational consequences, and evaluating compliance obligations. This ensures that the right resources are mobilized efficiently.

Regulatory reporting is central to incident escalation. Governments and industry regulators worldwide have mandated that organizations notify authorities when certain thresholds of compromise are met. For example, breaches involving personal data may trigger GDPR notifications in Europe, HIPAA reporting in healthcare sectors, or SEC disclosure requirements for publicly traded companies. AI assists by continuously evaluating which rules apply based on incident type, geographic scope, and organizational context. It automatically generates compliance reports, documenting what happened, what was compromised, and how the organization responded, ensuring accurate and timely reporting.

Multi-agency coordination adds another layer of complexity. High-profile incidents may involve national cybersecurity agencies, law enforcement, industry-specific regulators, and international task forces. AI systems can facilitate coordination by securely sharing incident data across authorized entities, ensuring that investigative, legal, and operational teams have access to consistent, verified information. These systems can also prioritize communications, identify relevant stakeholders, and generate briefings that synthesize technical findings into actionable insights for decision-makers.

Escalation management also involves stakeholder communication. AI can help craft incident notifications that balance transparency, legal obligations, and operational concerns. Automated tools may draft alerts for clients, employees, and partners, while flagging sensitive details that must remain confidential. Regulatory authorities expect clarity and precision, while the public demands accountability. Effective escalation ensures that communications do not inadvertently create additional liability or panic.

The technical response during escalation must scale accordingly. AI-driven systems must adapt to evolving threats, which may include lateral movement across networks, multi-vector attacks, or automated intrusion campaigns. Risk modeling continues to be critical, as AI predicts how the incident may propagate and identifies high-priority containment points. Forensic systems simultaneously capture evidence for ongoing investigation, regulatory reporting, and potential litigation. These processes operate at a speed and scale impossible for human teams to match without AI support.

Legal defensibility during escalated incidents is paramount. Regulators and courts scrutinize organizational decisions more rigorously when incidents have broad impact. Every mitigation step, communication, and reporting action is potentially subject to legal review. AI can log actions in real time, generate evidence chains, and provide auditors with traceable records of compliance. Organizations that integrate AI into escalation protocols not only improve their operational response but strengthen their legal position, demonstrating due diligence and proactive governance.

Finally, post-escalation review transforms incidents into strategic intelligence. AI systems analyze the response across all layers — technical, operational, legal, and regulatory — identifying what worked, where gaps existed, and how future responses can be improved. This analysis informs updates to policies, training, compliance frameworks, and predictive models, ensuring that organizations are better prepared for the next escalated incident. Escalation management is therefore not only about surviving a single event but evolving continuously, learning from each incident, and strengthening resilience in a world dominated by AI threats.

By integrating AI into every step of escalation — detection, reporting, coordination, response, and post-incident analysis — organizations gain a comprehensive framework for managing high-risk cyber events. AI provides speed, precision, and insight; human expertise provides judgment, ethics, and strategic oversight. Together, they enable organizations to navigate complex regulatory landscapes, coordinate across multiple agencies, and respond effectively to incidents that threaten critical assets, data integrity, and public trust. Escalation is no longer a reactive process but a structured, proactive strategy supported by predictive analytics, forensic intelligence, and legal foresight.

"The Night the Grid Went Dark"

It began as an ordinary Thursday night at MeridianGrid. The company's operations center was quiet, lights dimmed, and only the low hum of servers and cooling systems filled the room. SentinelShield, the company's AI monitoring engine, was already active, continuously analyzing terabytes of network traffic, system logs, and external threat feeds. At 1:13 a.m., it detected a subtle anomaly: minor irregularities in encrypted communications between remote data centers that, taken individually, appeared harmless. But SentinelShield recognized a pattern — an advanced AI intrusion was probing MeridianGrid's network, testing defenses, and laying the groundwork for a coordinated attack.

Within minutes, the AI predicted the potential impact. The intruder was capable of accessing sensitive financial data, manipulating transaction records, and disrupting operational systems across multiple global offices. SentinelShield initiated automated containment protocols: isolating high-risk endpoints, restricting network pathways, and creating forensic snapshots of critical systems. The incident was immediately classified as high severity, triggering escalation protocols. The AI determined that regulators, law enforcement, and key stakeholders would need to be informed within hours, not days.

By 1:47 a.m., the AI alerted the human operations team. They were stunned to find that the predicted escalation was no hypothetical scenario — the intrusion had already begun exploiting unpatched vulnerabilities in the logistics and finance modules. SentinelShield continuously updated its predictive models, simulating attack propagation and recommending real-time defensive actions. Automated scripts contained the intrusion in some systems, but others required human oversight to balance containment with business continuity. Decisions had to be made quickly: cut off critical systems to halt the intruder, or risk allowing the AI attack to spread further.

As MeridianGrid's executives were notified, legal teams prepared regulatory filings. AI-generated compliance reports detailed every step: the initial anomaly, the containment actions, forensic evidence collected, and mitigation strategies deployed. The company's reporting needed to satisfy multiple authorities simultaneously: the SEC, GDPR regulators for European clients, and national cybersecurity agencies in the United States. SentinelShield formatted reports for each jurisdiction, ensuring that technical findings, logs, and incident timelines were accurately translated into legally compliant documentation.

By 3:15 a.m., law enforcement was brought in. MeridianGrid coordinated with international cybersecurity task forces, sharing encrypted forensic data through secure AI-mediated channels. SentinelShield ensured that only authorized entities could access sensitive information, logging every access attempt. Investigators were able to trace the intrusion back to a network of AI agents operating across multiple continents, each with autonomous capabilities designed to bypass traditional security measures. It was a sophisticated operation that no human analyst could have unraveled alone.

The human and AI teams worked in tandem throughout the night. Engineers patched vulnerabilities, analysts reviewed AI-generated logs, and legal teams prepared notifications to clients and regulatory authorities. SentinelShield ran continuous simulations, anticipating how the attack could evolve, and adjusting containment measures in real time. By dawn, the immediate threat was neutralized, but the incident had left behind a trove of forensic evidence, detailing not only the intruder's actions but MeridianGrid's response at every moment.

In the weeks that followed, the incident became a landmark case study. Regulators praised the organization's transparency and swift action. SentinelShield's logs demonstrated that MeridianGrid had acted with due diligence, containing the attack efficiently and maintaining operational continuity. Lessons learned were integrated into updated risk models, escalation protocols, and AI training systems. The company had not only survived the attack but strengthened its defenses for the future.

The Night the Grid Went Dark became a defining moment for MeridianGrid. It was a demonstration of how AI could anticipate, contain, and document cyber incidents at unprecedented speed and scale. Humans and machines had worked in seamless coordination, navigating complex legal, regulatory, and operational challenges. In a world dominated by autonomous threats, the company learned that survival required not just defense, but foresight, coordination, and AI-powered intelligence that could escalate and resolve incidents with precision. The night ended not in disaster, but in a triumph of predictive strategy, legal compliance, and digital resilience.

Chapter 8

Post-Incident Analysis, AI Forensic Reviews & Continuous Improvement

In the aftermath of an AI-powered cyber incident, organizations face a critical phase that determines not only their future security posture but also their legal, regulatory, and operational credibility. Chapter 8 focuses on post-incident analysis, forensic review, and the continuous improvement cycle that follows every breach or near-miss. In the AI-driven cybersecurity landscape, this phase is no longer optional. Regulatory agencies, insurers, and stakeholders expect that organizations learn from incidents and implement measurable improvements to prevent recurrence. Effective post-incident analysis transforms crises into actionable intelligence, enhancing resilience and ensuring legal defensibility.

The first step in post-incident analysis is data consolidation. AI systems automatically collect logs, system snapshots, network traffic, access records, and endpoint activity into secure repositories. These datasets are often terabytes in size and contain millions of discrete events. AI-assisted forensic systems parse this data, identifying anomalies, correlating events, and reconstructing attack timelines. This level of granularity allows organizations to understand exactly what happened, how the breach unfolded, and which controls succeeded or failed. Post-incident analysis is no longer a matter of guesswork; it is evidence-driven and data-rich.

Next is root cause identification. AI forensic models analyze vulnerabilities, misconfigurations, and procedural gaps that enabled the intrusion. They assess whether the breach resulted from outdated software, mismanaged permissions, human error, or the evolving behavior of autonomous attackers. This analysis extends to third-party systems, cloud services, and vendor networks, ensuring that supply chain vulnerabilities are also considered. Identifying root causes enables targeted remediation and prevents recurrence, reducing both technical and legal risk.

Post-incident analysis also includes impact assessment. AI algorithms calculate the operational, financial, and reputational consequences of the incident. They quantify data exposure, potential regulatory fines, lost revenue, and customer impact. Predictive models can estimate how similar attacks might affect the organization in the future, creating risk profiles that guide decision-making. Organizations can then prioritize remedial measures based on potential impact rather than merely on perceived severity, ensuring resources are applied where they matter most. Another critical aspect is compliance verification. Post-incident analysis assesses whether the organization acted within regulatory and legal requirements during detection, containment, and response. AI systems automatically generate reports documenting actions taken, decisions made, and evidence collected, providing a defensible trail for regulators, auditors, and legal teams. This ensures that even in the face of a breach, the organization can demonstrate due diligence and adherence to standards, reducing liability exposure.

Continuous improvement is the final stage. Lessons learned are translated into actionable updates for security policies, AI monitoring algorithms, access controls, employee training, and operational workflows. AI-driven simulations can test these improvements by running hypothetical attack scenarios to evaluate their effectiveness. This creates a feedback loop: incidents inform improvements, improvements are tested, and outcomes are integrated into future predictive models. Organizations evolve continuously, ensuring that defenses remain adaptive against increasingly sophisticated AI threats.

Human oversight remains essential throughout this process. While AI excels at detecting patterns, reconstructing events, and identifying root causes, human experts interpret these outputs, make strategic decisions, and evaluate ethical and legal considerations. Security, legal, and operational teams collaborate to refine procedures, validate AI findings, and ensure that improvements align with organizational goals and compliance requirements.

Documentation is paramount. Every decision, mitigation step, and analysis finding must be securely recorded and easily auditable. AI systems can generate structured logs, reports, and executive dashboards, translating complex technical insights into actionable business intelligence. This ensures that the organization not only learns from incidents but can also demonstrate to stakeholders and regulators that it has done so responsibly.

Ultimately, post-incident analysis and continuous improvement transform cybersecurity from a reactive discipline into a proactive, adaptive strategy. Organizations that embrace AI-driven forensic review, rigorous root cause analysis, and iterative learning processes strengthen their defenses, reduce future risk, and enhance their legal and operational resilience. In an environment dominated by autonomous threats, survival is determined not only by prevention and response but by the ability to learn, adapt, and improve continually.

"The Day the Lessons Were Written"

It began with a quiet hum in the MeridianGrid operations center. Two days had passed since the company survived a sophisticated AI intrusion, and the immediate threat was neutralized. Systems were restored, networks stabilized, and clients reassured. Yet, the real work had just begun. SentinelShield, the AI forensic engine, had compiled terabytes of data capturing every movement of the intruder, every response by defensive systems, and every automated mitigation executed in real time. The team now faced the daunting task of transforming raw data into actionable lessons.

The post-incident review began at dawn. Analysts gathered around screens displaying dynamic timelines, anomaly heatmaps, and predictive attack simulations. SentinelShield presented the reconstructed sequence of events, showing how the intruding AI had navigated MeridianGrid's defenses, exploited a misconfigured cloud endpoint, and attempted to exfiltrate sensitive financial records. Every decision, delay, and containment action was recorded in millisecond detail. Human investigators marveled at the granularity — the AI had effectively created a story of the attack, complete with cause-and-effect relationships and predictive counterfactuals.

Root cause analysis revealed vulnerabilities that no one had noticed before. A third-party vendor had implemented an outdated security protocol that created a hidden pathway into the system. A rarely used administrator account had insufficient monitoring, allowing lateral movement. Even automated defensive rules had minor gaps that could have been exploited under different circumstances. SentinelShield highlighted each weakness, assigning risk scores and suggesting targeted remediation actions.

The next step was impact assessment. SentinelShield modeled the hypothetical consequences if the attack had progressed unmitigated. It calculated the financial cost, regulatory exposure, operational downtime, and reputational damage. The team was astonished by the insights. Had the intrusion extended just two more hours, millions of dollars would have been lost, regulatory penalties would have skyrocketed, and customer confidence would have eroded. The predictive modeling underscored the importance of rapid AI-driven mitigation.

Legal and compliance teams then reviewed SentinelShield's logs. Every containment action, alert, and forensic snapshot was presented in a structured, auditable format. Reports were generated automatically, demonstrating that MeridianGrid had followed internal policies and regulatory requirements at every stage. Even the regulators, who often scrutinize incident responses with microscopic detail, would find the documentation clear, defensible, and complete. For once, AI had not only protected systems but also protected the organization's legal standing. Continuous improvement sessions began immediately. SentinelShield simulated hundreds of potential future attacks, applying lessons learned from the recent incident. Network configurations were updated, endpoint monitoring rules tightened, and employee training programs revised to address new social engineering tactics. AI models were retrained with enriched datasets, improving their ability to detect anomalies and predict future threats. Every improvement was tested in simulated attack scenarios before implementation, ensuring that theoretical recommendations translated into real-world resilience.

The human team reflected on the collaboration with SentinelShield. Engineers, analysts, and compliance officers now understood that AI was not just a tool for detection but a strategic partner in learning and adaptation. Decisions were faster, insights were richer, and the organization could anticipate and respond to threats with unprecedented precision. The post-incident review had revealed not only vulnerabilities but also opportunities to evolve, innovate, and strengthen MeridianGrid's defenses.

By the end of the week, a comprehensive report was prepared for executives, stakeholders, and regulators. It documented the intrusion, the defensive response, the root causes, the impact assessment, and the improvements implemented. The lessons were written, not as abstract recommendations, but as actionable intelligence verified by AI analytics. MeridianGrid had not only survived the attack — it had transformed it into a catalyst for continuous growth and resilience.

The story became known internally as **"The Day the Lessons Were Written."** It was more than a post-mortem; it was a blueprint for the future. In a world dominated by autonomous threats, the organization had demonstrated that every incident, no matter how severe, could become a foundation for learning, legal defensibility, and operational excellence. SentinelShield had done more than preserve evidence; it had preserved the company's future, ensuring that knowledge gained would prevent disaster and empower proactive defense for years to come.

Chapter 9

Strategic Lessons, AI Governance & Future-Proof Cybersecurity

The AI-driven cyber landscape has permanently redefined the nature of risk, compliance, and organizational defense. Chapter 9 explores the strategic lessons organizations must internalize to thrive in a world where AI not only powers attacks but also governs investigations, audits, and regulatory enforcement. Beyond technical measures, cybersecurity is now deeply entwined with organizational governance, legal accountability, and continuous learning. The culmination of AI's role in cybersecurity is not just prevention or response; it is the creation of a resilient, future-proof framework that anticipates threats, manages risk, and adapts dynamically.

One of the first strategic lessons is that AI does not eliminate risk — it quantifies and mitigates it. Autonomous attacks, self-learning malware, and deepfake-enabled fraud are inevitable. Organizations must accept that breaches will occur and prepare systems and processes accordingly. AI models allow continuous risk assessment by assigning probability scores, mapping potential attack vectors, and simulating cascading failures. Risk is no longer theoretical; it is a quantifiable metric that drives governance decisions, investment priorities, and operational strategy.

Governance is central to AI cybersecurity. Boards of directors, executives, and risk committees must understand how AI systems make decisions, detect threats, and generate evidence. Policies must reflect both technical capabilities and regulatory obligations. Decisions about AI deployment, model training, access control, and incident response must be codified into governance frameworks that are auditable, defensible, and dynamic. Regulatory compliance is embedded within organizational policy, not treated as an afterthought. Organizations that fail to integrate governance into AI cybersecurity face amplified legal and reputational risks.

AI-driven evidence and forensic capabilities are crucial for strategic resilience. Post-incident analysis, root cause investigation, and predictive simulations provide data that inform governance decisions. Organizations can demonstrate due diligence, ethical decision-making, and regulatory compliance. Every logged event, anomaly detected, and response executed contributes to a permanent record. In legal or regulatory scrutiny, the ability to show proactive management and traceable decisions often determines organizational survival. AI not only uncovers breaches but also validates organizational behavior. Continuous improvement is another key lesson. AI allows organizations to implement iterative learning cycles after every incident. Simulations of attacks, scenario modeling, and predictive analytics inform policy refinement, technical upgrades, and human training. Lessons learned are codified into both AI algorithms and human procedures, ensuring that systems evolve to meet increasingly sophisticated threats. Organizations that fail to embrace continuous improvement risk obsolescence, as attackers continually adapt, and regulations evolve rapidly.

Strategic planning extends beyond internal operations. AI cybersecurity requires awareness of supply chain, third-party, and ecosystem vulnerabilities. Autonomous threats often exploit weak links in partner systems, vendor platforms, or shared networks. AI-based risk analysis extends across organizational boundaries, modeling exposure to third-party systems, regulatory jurisdictions, and geopolitical factors. Effective organizations integrate external risk assessment into governance, ensuring that strategies reflect the interconnected reality of modern digital ecosystems.

AI transparency and explainability are also essential. Regulatory authorities increasingly demand clarity on how AI models reach decisions, whether in threat detection, risk scoring, or forensic reconstruction. Black-box AI systems, no matter how technically sophisticated, create legal uncertainty. Organizations must maintain records, document model decisions, and provide human-understandable explanations of AI outputs. Explainable AI strengthens compliance, improves stakeholder trust, and provides legal defensibility when incidents are challenged in courts or regulatory hearings.

Finally, strategic cybersecurity is inseparable from organizational culture. Employees must understand that AI is a partner in defense, compliance, and evidence preservation. Human judgment complements AI insights, and ethical behavior, procedural adherence, and accountability remain essential. Strategic lessons are effective only if integrated into daily operations, training programs, and executive decision-making. Organizations that blend AI capability with governance, human oversight, and continuous learning achieve sustainable resilience.

The ultimate takeaway of AI-driven cybersecurity is that survival and success are not solely determined by preventing breaches, but by the ability to anticipate, respond, document, and learn. Governance, predictive risk modeling, forensic evidence, regulatory compliance, and continuous improvement form a unified strategy that transforms cyber risk from a reactive problem into a proactive opportunity. The organizations that internalize these lessons, integrate AI at every level, and maintain rigorous human oversight will not merely survive in the era of autonomous threats — they will thrive. AI cybersecurity is no longer just a function of IT; it is a strategic discipline, a governance challenge, and a continuous cycle of learning and adaptation.

"The Day the AI Became the Boardroom"

It was a Tuesday morning when MeridianGrid convened its quarterly executive review. The room was filled with directors, executives, legal counsel, and cybersecurity leadership. On the screens, SentinelShield — the company's AI monitoring and forensic engine — had prepared a comprehensive post-incident report covering the previous month's AI-driven attack attempts, near-misses, and system anomalies. The executives leaned forward as the AI began presenting insights that would have taken human teams weeks to assemble.

SentinelShield's first revelation was the predictive analysis of potential threats. The AI had simulated hundreds of attack scenarios, detailing which systems were most vulnerable and estimating potential financial and operational impact. It highlighted vulnerabilities that human teams had overlooked, traced attempted intrusions back to autonomous AI agents across multiple continents, and even predicted the timing and sophistication of future attacks. The executives were both awed and uneasy: the AI could foresee dangers with near-uncanny accuracy, surpassing human intuition. Next, the AI presented forensic reconstructions of recent incidents. It traced breaches with millisecond precision, documenting every unauthorized access, data transfer, and attempted exfiltration. For each event, SentinelShield provided a risk score, mitigation actions taken, and recommendations for policy changes. Legal counsel noted that every detail was auditable and compliant with regulatory requirements. The AI's work transformed complex, multi-layered cyber events into a narrative that was legally defensible and operationally actionable.

The discussion shifted to governance. SentinelShield had analyzed system behavior against organizational policies and regulatory frameworks, identifying gaps in compliance and suggesting improvements. It highlighted training needs for employees, updates required for third-party systems, and modifications to AI models themselves. The board realized that the AI was not just a technical tool — it had effectively become a member of the boardroom, providing strategic insights, legal context, and operational recommendations simultaneously.

Continuous improvement was another highlight. SentinelShield ran simulations of potential future attacks, using the organization's updated configurations to test defenses. It showed how different strategies could reduce risk, prevent data breaches, and improve regulatory compliance.

Executives discussed budget allocations, resource priorities, and procedural changes, guided by the AI's predictive analytics. Decisions that previously relied on human judgment alone were now informed by data-driven foresight, simulations, and risk modeling.

As the meeting progressed, the AI even provided scenario-based forecasting for regulatory changes and geopolitical risk. It mapped potential global cyber threats, modeled their impact on MeridianGrid's infrastructure, and suggested preemptive adjustments to policies and controls. It also highlighted how external vendors and supply chain partners could affect system resilience, prompting the board to consider contractual and operational changes. The AI's scope extended far beyond what a human team could monitor or analyze in a single review.

By the end of the session, the executives were in agreement: SentinelShield had shifted from being a monitoring tool to a strategic partner. Its insights informed legal strategy, risk management, operational planning, and governance decisions. Every recommendation was supported by data, simulations, and forensic evidence. The AI had become the ultimate advisor, capable of anticipating threats, guiding legal compliance, and improving organizational resilience before a single breach occurred.

The story spread through the company as a landmark example of AI-human collaboration. Employees realized that SentinelShield was not there to replace them but to amplify their capacity to protect the organization. Risk managers, legal teams, and IT operators embraced the AI's continuous feedback, integrating it into daily operations, training programs, and long-term strategic planning. The day the AI became the boardroom was remembered as a turning point: MeridianGrid had moved from reactive cybersecurity to proactive, strategic governance, guided by AI that learned, predicted, and advised at a scale unmatched by any human effort.

By the end of the quarter, the organization had transformed. Predictive models were updated, incident simulations were incorporated into training, and compliance dashboards were real-time and automated. SentinelShield continued to learn from every event, every anomaly, and every regulatory change, ensuring that MeridianGrid's defenses, governance, and legal preparedness were continuously evolving. In a world dominated by autonomous threats, survival depended not just on technology, but on strategic insight, foresight, and AI-guided governance. The AI had become the ultimate boardroom advisor — a permanent sentinel shaping decisions, reducing risk, and securing the organization's future.

Chapter 10

The Future of AI Cybersecurity: Autonomous Defense & Organizational Resilience

As organizations advance into an increasingly AI-driven digital ecosystem, the final frontier of cybersecurity is no longer solely reactive protection, but autonomous defense combined with strategic organizational resilience. Chapter 10 explores how the lessons of AI cyber risk, compliance, forensic intelligence, and governance converge to create a future-ready posture capable of anticipating and mitigating threats before they manifest. Autonomous defense, powered by machine learning, predictive analytics, and real-time risk modeling, represents the culmination of all previous strategies, transforming cybersecurity from a support function into a strategic organizational imperative.

The first principle of future AI cybersecurity is predictive anticipation. Autonomous systems continuously analyze vast amounts of internal and external data to identify emerging threats before they impact the organization. Unlike traditional monitoring, which reacts to anomalies after they occur, predictive AI examines behavior patterns, global threat intelligence, network flows, and user interactions to anticipate likely attack paths. By modeling potential adversarial moves and simulating responses, AI systems act as strategic sentinels, offering organizations a temporal advantage measured in milliseconds, minutes, or hours — potentially saving millions of dollars and critical assets.

Integration across governance, legal, and operational domains becomes essential. Autonomous AI systems not only detect threats but evaluate them in the context of regulatory obligations, internal policies, and contractual requirements. By continuously mapping incidents against jurisdiction-specific regulations, these systems ensure compliance while informing risk mitigation strategies. This integration allows boards, executives, and risk managers to rely on real-time, evidence-backed insights for strategic decision-making. Organizations are no longer limited to technical awareness; they gain operational clarity and legal foresight simultaneously.

Continuous learning is the cornerstone of AI-driven resilience. Every detected anomaly, contained intrusion, and forensic reconstruction feeds into self-improving algorithms, updating threat models, predictive simulations, and defense strategies. Post-incident reviews are automated, providing actionable intelligence for policy refinement, employee training, and infrastructure enhancements. Unlike static defenses, autonomous systems adapt dynamically, making them increasingly effective against evolving AI-powered attacks, including zero-day exploits, deepfake-enabled social engineering, and self-learning malware.

Autonomous response mechanisms are another defining feature of future AI cybersecurity. When predictive analytics identify a high-risk threat, the system can execute mitigation strategies without human intervention, including isolating compromised endpoints, throttling suspicious network traffic, adjusting access controls, and initiating automated backups. The speed and precision of AI responses reduce the window for potential damage dramatically, providing a level of operational resilience unattainable through manual processes alone. Human oversight remains crucial, ensuring that automated actions align with ethical standards and strategic priorities.

Forensic readiness is embedded at the core of autonomous cybersecurity. AI systems continuously log events, create tamper-proof evidence chains, and generate real-time compliance reports. These records are not simply reactive; they anticipate regulatory and legal scrutiny, ensuring that organizations are prepared for audits, investigations, and litigation. Autonomous systems capture both the technical and operational context, providing a comprehensive account of every decision, action, and anomaly, establishing a defensible record of due diligence.

Another strategic aspect is supply chain and ecosystem awareness. AI-driven risk models now incorporate external dependencies, including third-party vendors, cloud providers, and partner networks. Autonomous systems continuously evaluate vulnerabilities, simulate multi-organization attack scenarios, and predict cascading consequences of supply chain failures. This capability allows organizations to proactively manage third-party risks, adjust contracts, and enhance operational resilience across interconnected ecosystems, safeguarding against both direct and collateral damage.

Cultural integration is equally important. Autonomous cybersecurity must coexist with human decision-making, governance, and ethical considerations. Employees, executives, and risk managers are trained to interpret AI outputs, make strategic judgments, and act responsibly within the broader organizational context. Ethical AI ensures that autonomous actions comply not only with regulatory requirements but also with societal norms, fostering trust among stakeholders and ensuring long-term resilience.

Finally, future-proof cybersecurity relies on a feedback-driven strategic model. Continuous learning, predictive analytics, autonomous defense, and forensic intelligence form a unified cycle of improvement. Incidents inform simulations, simulations refine detection models, and detection informs governance and legal strategy. Organizations that internalize this feedback loop gain a sustained advantage over adversaries, demonstrating resilience, accountability, and adaptability in a rapidly evolving digital landscape.

In conclusion, the future of AI cybersecurity lies in uniting autonomous detection, predictive risk management, integrated governance, continuous learning, and legal defensibility. Organizations that embrace these principles will not only survive AI-driven attacks but thrive by converting threats into opportunities for strategic improvement. The evolution from reactive defense to proactive, autonomous resilience ensures that organizations remain secure, compliant, and adaptive, capable of navigating the complexities of an AI-powered world.

"When the Machines Took Command"

It was 3:06 a.m. when SentinelCore, MeridianGrid's next-generation AI cybersecurity platform, issued its first alert. Unlike previous incidents, this attack was unprecedented in speed, scope, and sophistication. An autonomous adversarial AI had infiltrated multiple systems, coordinating network scans, credential testing, and simulated insider activity across continents. Human operators could barely follow the flood of data. But SentinelCore had already begun predictive modeling, simulating thousands of potential attack vectors and anticipating each move with machine-level precision.

Within seconds, the AI initiated autonomous defensive measures. Vulnerable endpoints were isolated, suspicious network traffic was throttled, and encrypted backups were triggered. Even before the security team arrived, SentinelCore had reconstructed the attack timeline in real time, generating tamper-proof logs, forensic snapshots, and automated compliance reports. The system had effectively become the command center, managing both detection and response without human input.

When the operations team entered the room, the situation was extraordinary. Multiple screens displayed live simulations of attack scenarios, predictions of probable intrusions, and real-time risk scores for every critical system. SentinelCore projected the financial and operational impact of each possible outcome, prioritizing mitigation actions and adjusting strategies dynamically. Human analysts marveled at the AI's ability to coordinate defensive actions across offices, cloud environments, and global partners — it was orchestrating a symphony of protection that no human team could achieve.

The intruding AI adapted rapidly, attempting lateral movements, privilege escalation, and data exfiltration. SentinelCore anticipated each action, rerouting traffic, deploying countermeasures, and updating predictive models on the fly. Legal teams monitored alerts to ensure all responses aligned with regulatory frameworks, while compliance reports were automatically generated and timestamped for potential audits. The AI was simultaneously protecting assets, documenting evidence, and preparing the organization for any legal scrutiny.

By 4:30 a.m., the immediate threat had been neutralized. SentinelCore had captured every action of the intruder, reconstructed decision paths, and provided a complete forensic timeline. Even the attackers' AI signatures were analyzed, revealing coding patterns, operational behavior, and probable origin. The incident, while highly sophisticated, had been contained with minimal damage, all managed by a combination of autonomous AI response and human oversight.

Post-incident, SentinelCore ran hundreds of simulations to identify residual vulnerabilities and propose continuous improvement measures. Network configurations were updated, endpoint monitoring rules enhanced, and employee protocols refined. AI predictive models were retrained to detect similar attacks more rapidly. Lessons learned were translated into governance updates, compliance procedures, and strategic recommendations for board-level decision-making. The AI had not only defended the organization but had also strengthened its resilience for future threats.

The executives reviewed the incident report later that morning. SentinelCore's forensic evidence, predictive simulations, and risk analyses were comprehensive and auditable. Legal counsel confirmed that every regulatory requirement had been met, and compliance dashboards verified adherence to global cybersecurity standards. The organization's survival was not a matter of luck — it was a testament to autonomous intelligence, continuous learning, and integrated governance.

Over the following weeks, the story of "When the Machines Took Command" spread across the cybersecurity industry. MeridianGrid had demonstrated that in the age of autonomous threats, organizations could rely on AI not only to defend but to anticipate, document, and improve continuously. SentinelCore had become more than a defensive tool — it was a strategic partner, a predictive sentinel, and a legal witness. The incident proved that the future of cybersecurity was not reactive; it was autonomous, integrated, and continuously evolving, ensuring resilience in an increasingly complex digital world.

By the end of the quarter, MeridianGrid had institutionalized autonomous defense protocols, predictive risk modeling, and continuous improvement cycles across all departments. Employees understood that AI was both protector and advisor, guiding decision-making, anticipating threats, and preserving organizational integrity. "When the Machines Took Command" became a case study in forward-looking cybersecurity, illustrating that in a world dominated by autonomous adversaries, survival and success depended on foresight, adaptability, and strategic integration of AI intelligence at every level of the organization.

Final Thoughts

AI Cybersecurity in the Age of Autonomous Threats

The journey through *AI Cyber Risk, Compliance & Digital Forensics* has demonstrated a fundamental truth: cybersecurity is no longer solely a technical problem but a strategic, organizational imperative. Throughout the chapters, we have explored the multi-dimensional nature of AI-driven threats, from autonomous malware and AI-powered social engineering to deepfake attacks and zero-day exploits. The lessons are clear: in a world of intelligent, evolving adversaries, organizations cannot afford to be reactive. They must anticipate, detect, contain, and learn continuously, integrating technical, legal, and governance strategies into a cohesive defense framework.

Post-incident analysis and forensic reconstruction are no longer optional practices; they are critical mechanisms for survival. AI systems have the power to record every anomaly, every decision, and every mitigation step, creating a permanent, tamper-proof digital footprint. These records not only provide operational intelligence but are also essential for legal defensibility and regulatory compliance. Organizations that fail to implement AI-driven forensic readiness risk being unprepared for regulatory scrutiny, litigation, and reputational fallout. The future favors those who understand that the collection, interpretation, and preservation of evidence is as important as preventing breaches in the first place.

Continuous improvement is the linchpin of resilience. Each incident, whether minor or catastrophic, provides data that can inform future defensive strategies. Predictive modeling allows organizations to simulate potential attack scenarios, evaluate vulnerabilities, and prioritize remediation before the next incident occurs. Governance frameworks, when integrated with AI, ensure that organizational policies, human oversight, and ethical considerations remain aligned with technological capabilities. Regulatory compliance becomes part of the ongoing operational fabric, not an afterthought or static checklist. Organizations that embed continuous learning into their culture and systems gain a strategic advantage over adversaries, turning threats into opportunities for refinement.

Human oversight remains indispensable. AI can detect anomalies, reconstruct timelines, and simulate attack scenarios, but human experts interpret these insights, make judgment calls, and ensure that ethical and legal standards are maintained. The synergy between autonomous AI systems and skilled professionals is where organizational resilience emerges. Organizations that fail to integrate human insight into AI operations risk blind spots, misinterpretation, or over-reliance on opaque algorithms. AI is a tool, a sentinel, and a witness — but humans must govern its operation to maximize effectiveness.

Strategic lessons from this book highlight that cyber risk, compliance, and digital forensics are deeply interlinked. Boards, executives, IT teams, legal counsel, and compliance officers must collaborate seamlessly, guided by AI insights but unified under organizational objectives. Regulatory expectations, legal obligations, and operational realities must converge into a single, coherent strategy. Organizations that master this integration not only survive incidents but gain a sustainable advantage in trust, reputation, and operational excellence.

Future-proof cybersecurity requires anticipating threats that do not yet exist. Autonomous AI adversaries, deepfake campaigns, and global supply chain vulnerabilities demand systems capable of continuous learning, predictive defense, and multi-jurisdictional compliance. Organizations must deploy AI not merely as a shield, but as an intelligent partner that predicts, responds, and documents incidents, providing both operational security and legal defensibility. In essence, success is not measured by whether breaches occur, but by how effectively an organization prepares, responds, and evolves. The final takeaway is clear: AI has permanently changed the rules of cybersecurity. Defense is no longer reactive. Forensics are no longer manual. Compliance is no longer periodic. Legal defensibility, operational resilience, and continuous improvement are inseparable from AI-driven intelligence. The organizations that thrive are those that treat AI not only as a tool for threat detection, but as a strategic partner in governance, legal readiness, and proactive defense. Survival and success in the AI era depend on anticipation, adaptability, and the integration of technology, people, and policy into a cohesive, resilient system.

The future belongs to organizations that act strategically, document diligently, and learn continuously. AI cybersecurity is no longer just an operational function — it is a core pillar of organizational intelligence, resilience, and sustainability in the digital age.

www.ingramcontent.com/pod-product-compliance
Ingram Content Group UK Ltd.
Pitfield, Milton Keynes, MK11 3LW, UK
UKHW020157290926
15471UKWH00005B/923

9 798295 598555